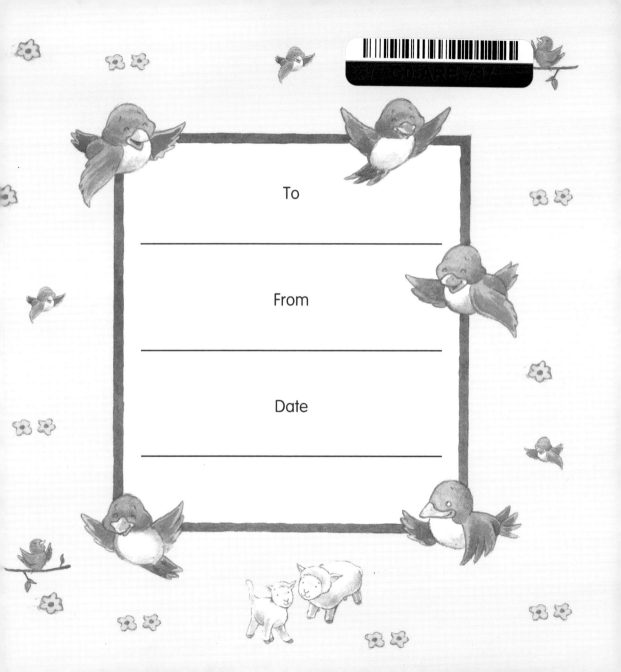

To

_____

From

_____

Date

_____

Psalms and Prayers for Little Ones

Allia Zobel Nolan

Illustrated by Tammie Lyon

HARVEST HOUSE PUBLISHERS
EUGENE, OREGON

For the all-loving, powerful, kind, gentle, merciful, and ever faithful God of the Psalms, for my husband, Desmond, whose steadfast encouragement never fails, for my nieces and nephews on both sides of the world, and for little ones everywhere, that they may learn, as the psalmists urged, to praise the Lord "from the rising of the sun until its going down" (Psalm 113:3 NKJV).

Allia Zobel Nolan

Psalms and Prayers for Little Ones

Text copyright © 2014 by Allia Zobel Nolan
Artwork copyright © 2014 by Tammie Lyon

Published by Harvest House Publishers
Eugene, Oregon 97402
www.harvesthousepublishers.com

ISBN 978-0-7369-5725-0

For more information about Allia Zobel Nolan, visit her at:
www.AlliaWrites.com

Design and production by Mary pat Design, Westport, Connecticut

Unless otherwise indicated, all Scripture verses are taken from *The Living Bible*, Copyright © 1971. Used by permission of Tyndale House Publishers, Inc., Wheaton, IL 60189 USA. All rights reserved.

Verses marked NLT are taken from the Holy Bible, New Living Translation, copyright © 1996, 2004, 2007 by Tyndale House Foundation. Used by permission of Tyndale House Publishers, Inc., Carol Stream, Illinois 60188. All rights reserved.

Verses marked NKJV are taken from the New King James Version®. Copyright © 1982 by Thomas Nelson, Inc. Used by permission. All rights reserved.

Printed in China

14 15 16 17 18 19 20 21 / LP / 10 9 8 7 6 5 4 3 2 1

For You, Little One

Because we love God, we want to learn all about him. Because God loves us, he has put that information in one place. Do you know where? On TV? Nope. In the movies? Nope. In the Bible? Yes.

The Bible is God's Word. It's a guidebook with everything we need to know to do God's will here on earth and make it to our final home in heaven. One of the most beautiful parts of the Bible is a section called "Psalms." This is a collection of poems, songs, prayers, and thoughts written to God or about him. Many were read or sung in the temple in Jesus' time. In fact, when Jesus was growing up, he learned the psalms and used them to pray. And you can too.

That's what this book is all about. To get you started, I've chosen some of my favorite psalms. I hope they will give you a better idea of what God is like, how he felt about his chosen people, how they felt about him, and how we can learn to trust him in good times *and* bad.

For Parents, Teachers, Grandparents, and Friends

"Children are a gift from the LORD," the Bible tells us. "They are a reward from him" (Psalm 127:3 NLT). While you can never fully repay God for the precious lives he entrusts to you, you *can* show your gratitude by teaching your little ones about him.

This book can be one of your tools. It will help you introduce youngsters to the Psalms. These beautiful scriptural writings show us a God who is a shield (Psalm 3:3), judge (Psalm 7:11), redeemer (Psalm 49:15), and more. They speak of his unfailing love (Psalm 48:9), mighty deeds (71:16), and loyal promises (Psalm 119:148). They also reveal the feelings God's people had as they worked through their relationship with their creator, sought answers to the human condition, and searched for ways to live a holy and God-centered life.

To make it easier for little readers, I chose and paraphrased several psalms that speak directly to their young life experiences and might inspire meaningful discussions.

Either while you're sharing these psalms with your little ones or after you're finished, reinforce what they've learned by using the "Digging Deeper" section and looking up the bolded words in the "Words and Their Meanings" section, which can be found in the back of this book.

Allia Zobel Nolan

Background

Have you ever wanted to tell God what's in your heart—feelings of happiness, sadness, or even anger? Have you ever wanted to shout, "Wow, God! You're the greatest! I love you," or say, "God, I'm afraid. Protect me," or ask, "God, why do bad things happen?" Many years ago, the shepherd and future king, David, the temple musician Asaph, the sons of Korah, and even Solomon wanted to say those same things. So they wrote them down.

Their writings were collected and became the part of the Bible called "Psalms." Another name for that collection is the **"Psalter."** There are 150 **psalms,** some of which may remind you of beautiful poems or prayers. Some were written to be read out loud or sung in the temple with music from flutes and **lyres.** And some are more like thoughts—the kind you might write in a diary titled "God and Me."

People who study the Bible believe David wrote most of the psalms (about 73) while he was a young shepherd tending his father's sheep or as a way to communicate with God as he grew older. As a group, David and the other authors are known as the **psalmists.** While many psalms are about personal experiences the writers had, others are about the kinds of ups and downs, questions, and situations we *all* have. They express joy, thanksgiving, praise, love, fear, and worry. They ask God for help with bullies, stress, anger, and forgiveness. Some are about feeling lonely, and some are about how many things don't seem fair.

Although those psalms were written a long time ago, they are just as important today. We use them to praise God, avoid sin, and restore a sense of calm and comfort on those not-so-great days. They are filled with just the right words—words we might not have been able to come up with ourselves—to tell God exactly what we are feeling. Because even though God already knows what's in our hearts, he wants to hear what we have to say.

So let's start now. Let's read, pray, and make the Psalms a part of each and every day.

Oh God, my heart is ready to praise you! I will sing and rejoice before you.
...For your **loving-kindness** is great beyond measure, high as the heavens.
Your faithfulness reaches the sky.

Psalm 108:6

The Happy Tree

God blesses those
who obey his rules and do the things he asks.
That means I don't join in with others who do wrong
or hang around with those who make fun of God.
Instead, I study my Bible
and think about ways I can get closer to God.
Yes! When I **avoid** what's wrong and do what's right,
I'm like a happy tree,
a tree planted near a cool, pure stream,
a tree that blossoms every year with fragrant flowers,
a tree that always gives tasty, ripe fruit.

Dear God,
help me always obey you, so I can
grow strong in your love and be
fruitful—like the happy tree.
Amen.

7

Psalm 8

God's Name

Everybody knows your name, God.

It's the greatest name on earth and in heaven.

And when I pray to you, God,

on summer nights when your stars twinkle

and your moon—like a gigantic ball of light—shines through my window,

I sit up in my bed and wonder,

Why is the Creator of the universe interested in me?

Then I remember it's because your love created me.

What's more, you put me (and everyone, even my little sister) in charge.

You handed over the whole world, everything you created—

birds, lambs, calves, wild animals, and all the fish in the ocean—

and told us to take care of it.

Wow! No wonder everybody knows your name, God.

You're awesome.

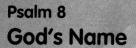

8

God,
remind me to use your name in the right way—with
respect—to praise, worship, sing, and talk to you.
Amen.

9

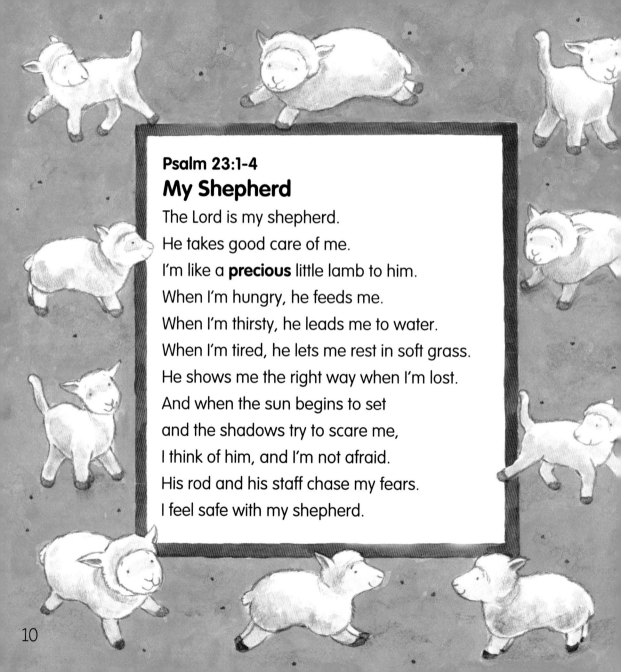

Psalm 23:1-4

My Shepherd

The Lord is my shepherd.

He takes good care of me.

I'm like a **precious** little lamb to him.

When I'm hungry, he feeds me.

When I'm thirsty, he leads me to water.

When I'm tired, he lets me rest in soft grass.

He shows me the right way when I'm lost.

And when the sun begins to set

and the shadows try to scare me,

I think of him, and I'm not afraid.

His rod and his staff chase my fears.

I feel safe with my shepherd.

Dear God,
the world is full of scary things, but you are more powerful than
any of them. Help me to remember I don't ever have to be afraid
with you by my side. I'm with my shepherd and he loves me.
Amen.

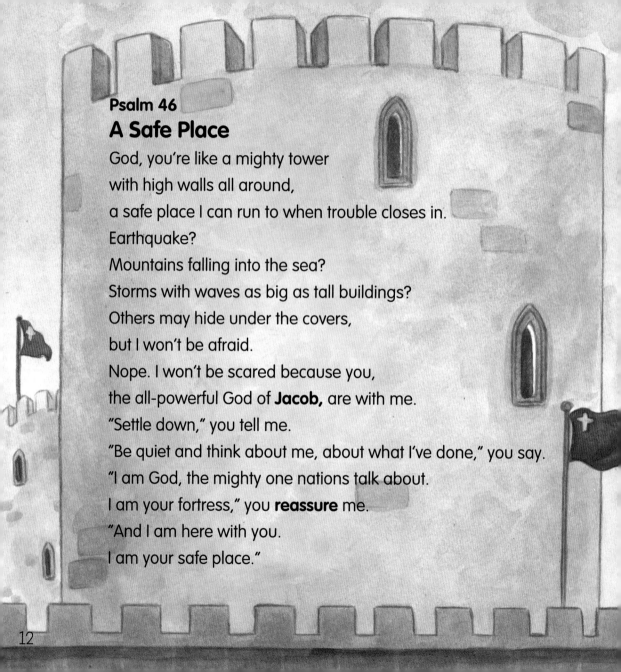

Psalm 46

A Safe Place

God, you're like a mighty tower
with high walls all around,
a safe place I can run to when trouble closes in.
Earthquake?
Mountains falling into the sea?
Storms with waves as big as tall buildings?
Others may hide under the covers,
but I won't be afraid.
Nope. I won't be scared because you,
the all-powerful God of **Jacob,** are with me.
"Settle down," you tell me.
"Be quiet and think about me, about what I've done," you say.
"I am God, the mighty one nations talk about.
I am your fortress," you **reassure** me.
"And I am here with you.
I am your safe place."

Dear God,
when I get upset and feel afraid, remind me to sit down, be quiet, take a deep
breath, and then think about all the things I *know* about you. You're loving and
kind and want only the best for me. After that, I'll feel fine.
Amen.

13

Psalm 73
God Is in Control

God is good. That's a fact.

But I forgot once.

It was when I saw others doing wrong and getting away with it.

I was jealous of them.

I thought, *Why do bad people have so much?*

I thought, *Does God even see what's going on? Is he paying attention?*

I was upset, so I went to the temple and prayed.

Then God opened my eyes.

He made me realize that he sees everything and knows everything

and will surely judge bad people in his own time,

and they will be punished for what they did.

I thought, *God sure is patient to stick with me even
when I complain.*

I thought, *Others may have lots of toys, but those things can't
compare with God. They will not last, but God will always be with me.*

Finally I thought, *I see everything clearly now. It's silly to want anything but God.*

Dear God,
help me to remember that I may not have as many toys or
goodies as some people who don't follow your ways. But I have
something much, much better. I have you. Amen.

15

Psalm 104
All I Need

God, you're the greatest!

You're the king of all creation.

You set the earth on firm ground,

and then watered it with springs and rivers,

so wild animals have a place to come and drink.

You planted trees that reach to the sky,

so birds can build their nests and take care of their babies.

You carved out miles of ocean beds,

so whales and dolphins can leap and dance

and seahorses and crabs can play hide-and-seek.

You filled the earth with food,

so people, animals, insects—every living creature—can eat.

Yes, God, you're the greatest, and I will tell you that all of my life!

You give us the air we breathe and the bread we eat.

You give us all we need.

Dear God,
you created us all. And you care for us all. So,
remind me next time I come to you asking for
things that I don't always need more of that I can
never praise you enough for giving me just the
right amount—all I need.
Amen.

17

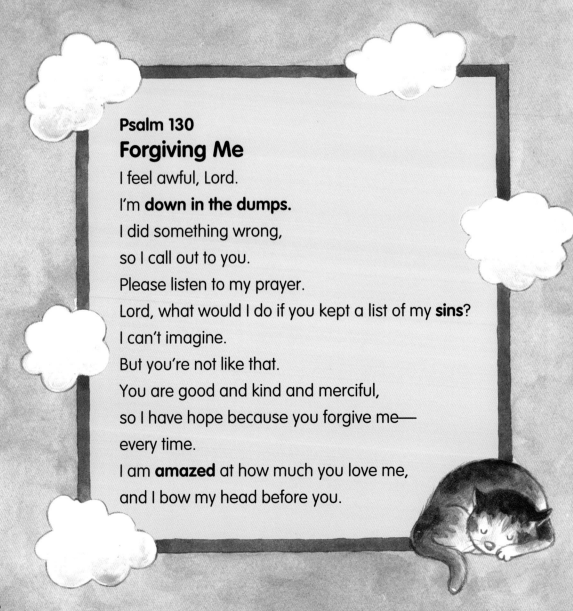

Psalm 130

Forgiving Me

I feel awful, Lord.

I'm **down in the dumps.**

I did something wrong,

so I call out to you.

Please listen to my prayer.

Lord, what would I do if you kept a list of my **sins**?

I can't imagine.

But you're not like that.

You are good and kind and merciful,

so I have hope because you forgive me—

every time.

I am **amazed** at how much you love me,

and I bow my head before you.

Dear God,
you always forgive me when I ask you to. And even when I don't ask, you forgive me. Please help me to remember that when it's my time to forgive others. In Jesus' name, I pray. Amen.

Psalm 133

Togetherness

Isn't it nice
when brothers and sisters and friends
(even boys and girls who've just met)
play peacefully, giggle, and get along?
When children of God
(that's you and me) share and help each other,
when we are like one, big family,
it's as sweet as the perfume used to anoint a holy man
or as satisfying as the **dew** that waters the plants on a holy mountain.
Togetherness is a blessing.

20

Dear God,
when Jesus was on earth, he gathered people together, so they could
worship you and help each other. That's called "being in community."
Help me be in community with others...so we can all do your will.
Amen.

21

Psalm 139:1-16
One Special Me

Thanks, God, for making me.

Thanks for all the time you spent thinking about what I'd be like.

When I was being formed, when my bones and skin, hair and eyes,

and even the sparkle in my eyes were coming together,

thanks for making sure they were just right.

Oh and, Lord, thanks for carefully arranging all the days of my life in your book too.

Wow! With all you have to do,

I'm **amazed** that you think about me a zillion times a day,

all through the night, and then again when I wake in the morning.

That's a lot of thinking.

All I can say is I must be very special to you.

Dear God,
sometimes I feel I'm not as tall, pretty, or smart as some kids.
Help me stop comparing myself to others and remember you
made me with care and love just the way I am—on purpose.
Amen.

Psalm 141
I Need Help, God!

Help! Quick! Save me!

Close my mouth, God, so it doesn't make me sin.

Protect my heart so I won't be tempted to do or say bad things.

I don't want to do or say anything mean.

I don't want to use a bad word.

I don't want to fall in with boys and girls who make fun of others
or gossip or say rude things.

Keep me from them, God.

And if I slip, do wrong, and get scolded, that's okay, God.

I know that it is for my own good.

In the meantime, God, please be my protector.

Please help me to keep my eyes fixed on you, and

help me **sidestep** those who are trying to make me sin.

Let them fall into their own traps.

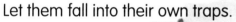

Dear God,
it's great to know I can run to you for help when people try to get me
to say or do things that are wrong. Thanks for being my protector.
Amen.

Psalm 150

Praise the Lord

Hallelujah, everybody!

Let's praise the Lord.

Let's praise him in our country churches.

Praise him in his heavenly home.

Praise him for the wonderful things he's done.

Let's sound the trumpet,

strum the guitar,

and blow hard on the flute.

Let's bang the drum, crash the cymbals,

and tap out music with our feet.

Let's you and I and every creature,

great and small, let's all

praise the Lord!

Dear God,

If I spent my whole life praising you—telling you how wonderful, powerful, great, and mighty you are—that still wouldn't be enough. But it's a start, and so I'm going to begin today.

Amen.

Digging Deeper

Now that you've read a few of the psalms, let's see how much you remember. The answers are on the opposite page.

Questions:

1. When we do what's right, what are we like? **a)** an angel

   b) a "happy" tree that bears lots of fruit

   c) one of the disciples

2. Whose name is known all over the world?

3. In Psalm 23, what is God compared to? **a)** tower

   b) shepherd

   c) mountain

4. Name two things we can do when we are upset or worried.

5. True or false. People who do bad things and don't get caught are lucky.

6. True or false. God always gives us everything we ask for right away.

7. How many times does God forgive us? **a)** ten times

   b) one hundred times

   c) every time

8. True or false. Togetherness means we join others in doing God's will.

9. Yes or no. We are not as special as our friends who can sing really well.

10. What can we do when we're tempted to say a bad word or make fun of someone?

11. True or false. We can only praise God in church.

Answers:

1. When we do what's right, we are like (b) a "happy" tree that bears lots of fruit (Psalm 1).

2. The name that is known all over the world—the name above all others, the name we should only say in prayer and praise—is God. Even if others do, we should never use God's name carelessly (Psalm 8).

3. In Psalm 23, we compare God to a (b) shepherd who loves and takes care of his sheep (Psalm 23).

4. When we are upset or worried, we can stop, be quiet, and then think about what we know about God. He loves us. He has always helped us in the past and will help us with whatever our problem is now (Psalm 46).

5. False. People who do bad things and don't get caught are not lucky. They may have gotten away with behaving badly here on earth, but they will have to answer to God, who will judge everyone at the end of time (Psalm 73).

6. False. God may not give us the latest gadget or toy, but he will give us everything we truly need (Psalm 104).

7. God forgives us (c) *every* single time we sin if we are sorry and ask him to (Psalm 130).

8. True. When we gather with others and go to church, help feed the poor, take care of people without homes, or tell people about God, we are together in doing God's will (Psalm 133).

9. No. God made us special. He loves us just the way we are. What's more, before we were even born, he wrote all about us in his book (Psalm 139).

10. When we are tempted, be quick to call on God, our protector. We can ask him to keep us from bad things and bad people who will try to lead us to sin (Psalm 141).

11. False. We can praise God in church, in the bedroom, on the school bus, when taking a walk, and while watching a beautiful rainbow. In fact, we can praise God anywhere and anytime (Psalm 150).

Words and Their Meanings

A

avoid: to stay away from someone or something, or to not do something

amazed: to be surprised or filled with wonder by something or someone

D

dew: tiny drops of water that form in the night on plants and grass after the air has cooled

down in the dumps: feeling sad or in a bad mood

H

hallelujah: a word or song meaning "praise be to God" used to thank God

J

Jacob: the son of Isaac and Rebekah, the brother of Esau, and the grandson of Abraham and Sarah (You might remember that in the story from Genesis 5:15-27:41, Jacob tricked his brother, Esau, and took the blessing that should have gone to him.)

L

loving-kindness: being nice or kind to someone because you love them

lyre: a stringed object like a harp that people used to make music with in Bible times

P

precious: when someone or something is worth a lot or loved very much

psalm: sacred songs, poems, or prayers, many of which are in the Bible's book of Psalms

psalmists: the name given to the people who wrote biblical psalms—David, Asaph, Solomon, and Moses

Psalter: another name for the book of Psalms

R

reassure: to tell someone they don't have to worry about something so they are not afraid or nervous

respect: to treat a person in a way that shows you think good things about them

S

sidestep: to get out of the way of someone or something

sin: choosing on purpose to do something, think something, or behave in a way that is against God's rules

Sing a new song to the Lord!
Sing it everywhere around the world!
Sing out his praises! Bless his name.
Each day tell someone that he saves.
Publish his glorious acts throughout the earth.
Tell everyone about the amazing things he does.

Psalm 96:1-3